Stuff I'd Only Tell God

Faithful Forever!

[signature]

2024

Stuff I'd Only Tell God

A GUIDED JOURNAL
OF COURAGEOUS HONESTY, OBSESSIVE TRUTH-TELLING, AND BEAUTIFULLY RUTHLESS SELF-DISCOVERY

Jennifer Dukes Lee

BETHANYHOUSE
a division of Baker Publishing Group
Minneapolis, Minnesota

© 2023 by Jennifer Dukes Lee

Published by Bethany House Publishers
Minneapolis, Minnesota 55438
www.bethanyhouse.com

Bethany House Publishers is a division of
Baker Publishing Group, Grand Rapids, Michigan

Printed in the United States of America

ISBN 978-0-7642-4167-3 [paperback]
ISBN 978-0-7642-4210-6 [casebound]
ISBN 978-1-4934-4246-1 [ebook]

Cover design by Micah Kandros Design

The author is represented by Alive Literary Agency, aliveliterary.com

Baker Publishing Group publications use paper produced from sustainable
forestry practices and post-consumer waste whenever possible.

23   24   25   26   27   28   29   7   6   5   4   3   2   1

Contents

Dear You   7

Before You Begin   11

1. Me and My People   13

2. Me and My Past   45

3. Me and My Right Now   79

4. Me and My Weird Ways   113

5. As Honest As I've Ever Been   147

6. Me and My Future   183

7. Finally   217

Dear You

Hello there, new friend.

My name is Jennifer, and I am about to become the nosiest friend you will ever have.

My parents tell me that one of my favorite words as a little girl was *Why?* At dinner parties, my friends get nervous when I lean forward over a table to ask, "So, can you tell me how you *really* feel about . . . ?"

I have always loved good questions, even making a career out of asking them as a news reporter.

I don't ask questions to pry or to annoy people. I'm mostly just . . . curious. People are astonishingly interesting to me. *You* are astonishingly interesting to me.

We can learn a great deal by paying attention to whatever comes after the beautiful curve of a question mark.

Yet, for many years, I quietly struggled with a long list of questions that seemed unanswerable. It's as if the answers were hidden in locked rooms with missing keys. They were questions about the universe, myself, stupid things from my past, injustice, and the existence of God. They were the kinds of questions that kept me awake at night:

What's the purpose of my life?
Why am I the way I am?
How do I leave my past in the past?
Am I the only one this weird?
Will I ever be enough?
How can I do better tomorrow?

I began to look to God for answers, interrogating him in the same way that I interrogated police chiefs, presidential candidates, and unsuspecting dinner guests. What I found awakened me to the unrelenting love of God, who has never indicated a distaste for my questions.

Here's what I know to be true: life will never make sense until we get curious enough to ask good questions.

And so, I created this journal for you. In *Stuff I'd Only Tell God*, I pulled together daring, quirky, thought-provoking, silly, and soul-searching questions to ask yourself. It's the stuff I'd ask you if you invited me to a dinner party—and I'd invite you to ask them of me as well.

This journal will ask something of you, namely *courageous honesty and obsessive truth-telling*.

Honesty feels vulnerable and scary, like walking into a room without pants on. Honesty takes a special kind of courage, and ultimately, it holds a special kind of power. It is a form of intimacy with yourself—and with God.

That's why this journal exists: to give you a place for the most transparent truth-telling of your life. Think of it as your own little confessional booth.

Here, you will push your limits of vulnerability and self-reflection. You will plumb your own depths and your own history. You will understand what makes you tick—and what ticks you off. You will remember your past and reimagine your future. This journal offers you space to write down the stuff you believe to be true, and the "truths" you've reconsidered. It's a place to record your ideas and memories and preferences that might seem outlandish or outrageous to someone else—but they're the things that make you *you*.

Ultimately, this journal is a brand-new path in front of you. But this is more than a path to walk; it's one to blaze. The adventure before you is one you are charting, with great personal courage—and with God, who is intimately familiar with the ways that you take.

High-level honesty can be a humbling thing, but this type of inner work will help you treat yourself more kindly, more empathetically. In the end, this beautifully ruthless work could change the way you feel about other people—and the way you feel about God, too.

Before you begin, you have an important question to ask yourself:

"Do I have the courage to write down the stuff I'd only tell God?"

Your yes *might be the bravest* yes *you'll ever give.*

Before You Begin

Step 1: *Commit to ruthless honesty and generous compassion.* When you combine these two virtues, you end up with a more complete and charitable view toward yourself and others.

Step 2: *Choose your adventure.* This journal is structured in a particular order, starting with your people, because the people in your life have a tremendously powerful influence on your past, present, and future. The journal then guides you on a journey through your past, your right now, and your weird ways. Next, you deep-dive into your most protected secrets in the section titled "As Honest As I've Ever Been." Finally, you'll give yourself space to dream about what you want your future to look like, so you can make each day count from here on out. Feel free to start wherever you choose. *Just start.* This is your adventure.

Step 3: *Upon completion, determine what's next.* What will you do with this little book of secrets? You can hide it, bury it, burn it, trash it, papier-mâché it, mulch it, shred it, allow the dog to chew on it, rip it up, or put it in a time capsule with strict instructions that it not be read until 2052. Or, you might just feel emboldened enough to share the stuff you'd only tell God . . . with someone else after all.

Me and My People

You are the sum of a lot of things: your parents' DNA, your personality, your culture, your choices, your habits, your victories, and your struggles.

You are also shaped by every person who's been a part of your life, every person who's cared for you, every person who's hurt you, every person who's prayed for you, every person who's abandoned you, and every person who's loved you. Sometimes people are with you for a day, some are with you for a season, and some are with you for a lifetime. Each one leaves an imprint on the person you are becoming.

When you take time to think back on those souls, you can learn a lot about why you are the way you are. You can also learn a lot about the kind of human you want to be from here on out.

It can take a good bit of courage to encounter some of those people on the pages ahead, especially if they've hurt you, or if you can never see them again. But this exploration is part of your healing and central to your becoming.

As the faces and names emerge, some of them will bring you sorrow. And some will bring you unanticipated joy. You'll remember the way they made you laugh and how they looked after you. You'll remember the secrets you've shared, the promises they've broken, and the forgiveness that has brought you this far. Take a moment with each soul, remembering the mark they made on you and the mark you made on them.

These are your people.

The Central Repository of All the People Who Have Been a Part of My Life

The Central Repository of All the People Who Have Been a Part of My Life

Time for a brain dump. Fill these pages with every person you can think of who has influenced your life, for better or for worse.

My Class Yearbook Superlatives

Have you ever seen those pages in yearbooks where high school students voted for each other based on their various attributes? *Best hair. Most athletic. Most likely to succeed.* They're called "yearbook superlatives."

For a moment, let's say the people in "The Central Repository of All the People Who Have Been a Part of My Life" made up an entire high school class. Now it's your turn to assign the yearbook superlatives to the "class" that is your life. Your vote is the only one that counts.

Most Unique _____

Most Likely to be on a Reality Show _____

Most Likely to Ride a Mechanical Bull _____

Best Dressed _____

Most Misunderstood _____

Kindest _____

Most Humble _____

Most Likely to Pray for Me _____

Most in Need of Prayer Right Now _____

Human Encyclopedia _____

Most Likely to Cry When They Run Over a Turtle with Their
   Car _____

Most Gullible _____

Most Likely to Shop at Walmart _____

Most Likely to Shop at Trader Joe's _____

Teacher's Pet _____

Has No Filter _____

Worst Driver _____

Someone I Could Bring Home to the Parents _____

Knows the Lyrics to Every Song _____

Biggest Hoarder _____

Most Likely to be Famous Someday _____

Hardest Working _____

Quirkiest _____

Most Environmentally Conscious _____

Most Imaginative _____

Best Problem Solver _____

Most Understanding _____

Biggest Potty Mouth _____

Best Laugh _____

Most Likely to Keep a Secret _____

Most Likely to Share My Secrets _____

Best Cook _____

Class Clown _____

Most Likely to Run Out of Gas _____

Most Unforgettable _____

Life of the Party _____

Who's got your six? WWI pilots came up with the phrase *got your six* in reference to the rear of an airplane—the six o'clock position. As a pilot, the six is what's behind you. It's the most vulnerable part of your plane. So, when someone tells you they've "got your six," it means they've got your back.

This is who's got my six

This is whose six I've got

This is who makes me laugh the loudest

No matter how long it's been, I can always pick up where I left off with this person

Right now, the person I trust most is

The two people I struggle most to love are

The best friend I've ever had is

The friend I miss most is

The person I can't wait to see when I get to heaven is

My most influential teacher was

These are a few people who make me feel whole

These are a few people who make me feel worthless

I smile every time I think about this person from my childhood

These are four people I want to reach out to who I haven't spoken to in a while

God loves everybody. I especially need to remember that when I think about this person

This is who makes me cry sad tears

This is who makes me cry happy tears

This is who makes me cry mad tears

This is a person who turned out to be different than I originally thought (good or bad)

I understand God best because of these people

A person who understands God better because of me

I am looking out for the people in my life by

I can see how God was at work when he put this person in my life

LOST IN TRANSLATION

A beautiful feature of language is that it gives us the vocabulary to describe what we're feeling and a way to express ourselves with precision. The English language includes thousands upon thousands of words, but sometimes there isn't a perfect, succinct English word for what we feel. Our friends around the world are here to help. Here are some words for which there are no English equivalents, but you'll know exactly what they mean when you read the definitions, because you've probably experienced them. You'll find a few of these "Lost in Translation" sections throughout this journal, starting here:

> *Retrouvailles*, **French**
> *Retrouvailles* describes the happy feeling you get when reuniting with someone you love after a long time.

I felt *retrouvailles* when I reunited with

LOST IN TRANSLATION

Pena ajena, **Spanish**

Pena ajena is the embarrassment you feel due to someone else's behavior or actions.

I experienced *pena ajena* when

Ya'aburnee, **Arabic**

Ya'aburnee translates literally to "you bury me." It's the hope you have that you'll die before someone you love because life on earth would feel unbearable without them.

I feel *ya'aburnee* about this person/these people

LOST IN TRANSLATION

> ### *Farginen,* Yiddish
> *Farginen* is a word that means to wholeheartedly delight in someone else's success or delight. It's the opposite of envy.

I had a sense of *farginen* for

This person is someone I know who consistently exhibits *farginen*

This was a time in my life when I wish I had exhibited *farginen* but didn't

LOST IN TRANSLATION

Razbliuto, Russian
Razbliuto is that sentimental feeling you get toward someone you once loved but no longer do.

I feel a sense of *razbliuto* every time I think of this person

Iktsuarpok, Inuit
Iktsuarpok is the feeling you get when you're so eager for someone to arrive, you keep looking outside (or going outside) to see if they've made it yet.

I had major *iktsuarpok* going on when I was waiting for

and this is why

LOST IN TRANSLATION

> **Koi no yokan, Japanese**
> Koi no yokan is a premonition you have, when you first meet a person, that the two of you are going to fall in love.

Pick one:

I've had *koi no yokan*, and here's how I knew

I haven't had *koi no yokan* yet, but this is why I believe it's possible

I don't believe in *koi no yokan*, and this is why

LOST IN TRANSLATION

Mamihlapinatapai, Yaghan

Mamihlapinatapai is a look that you share with another person when you are both wishing that the other person would do something you both desire, but neither is willing to start.

I experienced *mamihlapinatapai* with _____
when

Gattara, Italian

Gattara is a title reserved for women who take care of cats. In fact, they probably prefer spending time with felines more than humans. Think "crazy cat lady."

I know a *gattara*, and her name is

The most important people in my life, in no particular order

1. _____

2. _____

3. _____

4. _____

5. _____

6. _____

7. _____

8. _____

9. _____

10. _____

I need better boundaries with this person

I would hate if this person got their hands on this journal, or my diary

I vow to do better with the people in my life by
(circle the ones that apply):

Forgiving more

Having more fun

Going first

Being the inviter

Being kinder

Saying yes

Saying no

Praying when I say I will

Assuming others have good intentions

Listening

Lightening up

Giving people the benefit of the doubt

Showing gratitude

Putting my phone down

Being more flexible

Sacrificing

Laughing

Admitting I'm wrong

Showing up

Being available

Looking people in the eye

Decreasing the sarcasm

Offering the gift of touch

What I Wish People Knew about Me

I hope I don't get stranded on an island with

In heaven, I want to live next to

When I think about the members of my family, I am
most like

When I think about my friends, I am most like

My Big-Screen Adaptation

If my life were a movie, here is the actor who would play the part of me

The name of the movie would be

These are the actors who would play the other characters and the names of people in my life they are portraying

The ten qualities I want most in a friend are

1.

2.

3.

4.

5.

6.

7.

8.

9.

10.

Here are five times I've been a really good friend

1. _____

   _____

2. _____

   _____

3. _____

   _____

4. _____

   _____

5. _____

   _____

The person in my life who knows me best

The person in my life who doesn't really know me at all

One person I'd love to bring back to life on earth is

Let's Make a Genogram

A genogram is kind of like a psychological family tree where you diagram the history of behaviors, personalities, and tendencies. Then you study the interplay of generations and consider what it could mean for you and your possible descendants. On the following pages, diagram your family and include any details (good and bad) about repetitive behaviors, personalities, habits, etc. Did or does anyone in your family struggle with depression? Alcoholism? Unfaithfulness? But don't just dwell on the bad. Who was particularly faithful to God? Who has a rich prayer life?

Add extra pages in a separate journal, as needed, to make room for aunts, uncles, siblings, and other people whose behaviors, personalities, and tendencies are noteworthy.

Let's Make a Genogram

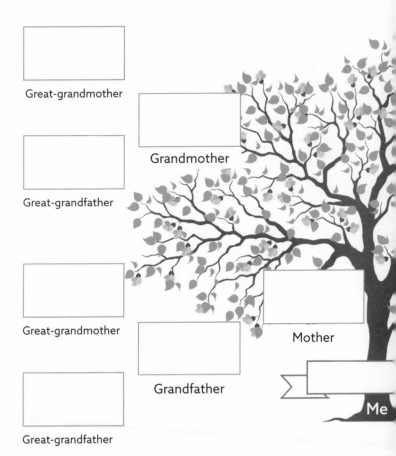

Great-grandmother

Grandmother

Great-grandfather

Great-grandmother

Mother

Grandfather

Great-grandfather

Me

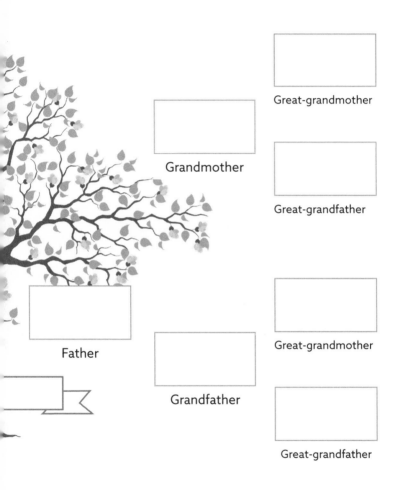

Great-grandmother

Great-grandfather

Grandmother

Great-grandmother

Great-grandfather

Father

Grandfather

Let's Make a Genogram

What patterns do I see in my genogram?

What do I want to carry forward?

What cycles do I want to stop?

Let's Make a Genogram

This is my plan to take action in my life, based on the results of my genogram

I need help forgiving these people

I need to ask for forgiveness from these people

This is what I need to say about my mom

This is what I need to say about my dad

Spending the rest of my life with one person sounds

The person who has given me the best advice is

I wish I would've said what I needed to say to this person

. . . and this is what I wish I would have said

God made me the kind of person who

Me and My Past

Every once in a while, you have to look back before you step forward. You need to pause and examine the decisions and circumstances that have brought you to this point in your life. That's the sort of thing that will serve you well as you move into your future.

You don't have to live in the past, but it's a good idea to look at it. If your past were a patch of earth, you'd see holes and you'd see gardens.

First, the holes. Holes pockmark the soil of your life. They are empty, gaping. Inside these holes, you feel real pain from the jagged spades that dug them. And if you're honest with yourself, you haven't processed those emotions like you probably should. You've got regrets. You wish you could have handled some things differently. There are wounds inflicted on you, and wounds you inflicted on others.

Some of these holes were ones you dug yourself. But those holes are not the end of you. If you look closely, they are places of beginning. In these holes, you can plant new seeds . . . and watch something bloom again one day.

And then there are gardens.

The gardens are the places where good memories have grown. You will see how you were blooming in the exact way you were meant to bloom. Sometimes people saw the beauty unfolding, and sometimes no one knew but you and God.

When you scan the horizon of your life, you can see how you grew something glorious and colorful from the tiniest seeds. Day by day, the growth was nearly imperceptible, but now when your eyes sweep the landscape, you see it all more clearly than you ever did before.

Gardens and Holes

See the previous page for definitions of gardens and holes.

These are the holes in the soil of my life

Gardens and Holes

These are my gardens

The three best moments of my life are

This is the part of me that has changed the most over the years

God has healed

I don't understand why God hasn't healed

I hope that this journal doesn't make me write about this

Ups and Downs

Write the years or decades of your life, evenly distributed, on the lines provided at the bottom of the graph on the following page. Plot the happiest and saddest seasons of your life on it, with the happiest seasons at the top and the saddest at the bottom.

Ups and Downs

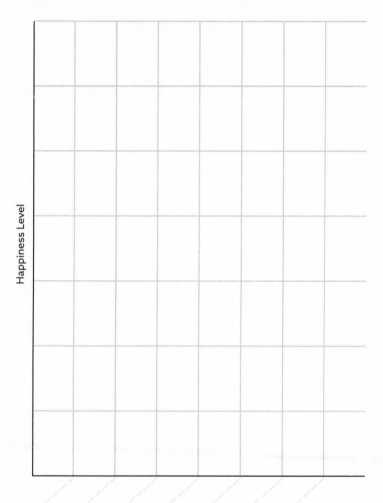

Happiness Level

Years or Decades of Life

Ups and Downs

When I look at my life on the Ups and Downs graph,
I notice how

A time something went better than I thought it would

The five most beautiful things I've ever made

1. _____

2. _____

3. _____

4. _____

5. _____

When I was a child, I dreamed that I would become

When I look back on my life, the thing I regret the most is

This is the best news I've received in . . .

the last month

the last year

the last decade

Dear Younger Me

This is what I'd tell my ten-years-ago self

Dear _____ ,

_____

_____

_____

_____

_____

_____

_____

_____

_____

_____

_____

_____

_____

_____

_____

_____

A childhood tradition that I cherish

A childhood food that I loved

My favorite school lunch

My childhood pets (or the pets I wish I had—or the pets I never wanted)

A childhood best friend

Are we still friends? Y or N

My favorite pastimes as a kid

My favorite place to go alone when I was a kid, to think or to cry

If I could bring back one restaurant from my past, this would be the one

The time I felt closest to God was when

The time I felt farthest from God was when

The last time I cried was

The last time I laughed was

Your Life, In Just Six Words

Legend has it that Ernest Hemingway was once asked to write a story using only six words. The novelist responded, "For sale: baby shoes, never worn." Your life story could fill a whole book, but sometimes all you need is a handful of words.

Here's my six-word memoir

This is the struggle that most shaped who I am today

These are the three things I wish I'd done differently in my life

Here's a list of things God has redeemed

Promises, Promises

These are the promises I've kept

These are the promises I shouldn't have broken

A promise I'm glad I broke

The hardest promise I've ever kept

Turning Points

We all have moments in our lives when everything shifts and we find ourselves turned in a new direction. Sometimes, the uncharted path ahead looks bright with possibility. Other times, it looks daunting in its unfamiliarity. Often, we don't recognize how important these shifts are until months or years later, when we deliberately turn around and shine a spotlight on the places our feet once roamed. Then we see those moments for what they truly are: turning points.

A turning point in my faith

A turning point in my career

A turning point in my family

Turning Points

A turning point in my attitude

A turning point in my health

Here's a path I didn't take that only makes sense now

I would never want to change this, even though it felt bad/
uncomfortable/weird/disappointing at the time

The biggest crossroads of my life

The worst advice I ever got

The best advice I ever got

These are the lies I have told

These are the lies I have been told

.

I wish I would've been kinder to

I will forgive

God, I don't understand why

I felt most loved when

A Wave of Nostalgia

You taste a cinnamon roll, and you are transported to your grandma's kitchen. You hear a love song, and suddenly, the affection you felt comes rushing in once more. The sweet scent of pink lotion fills a room, and you instantly remember the baby you held in your arms. Deeply ingrained pathways in our brains connect our senses to days gone by. Take a moment to let your senses show you the way back.

When I smell _____ I remember

When I taste _____ I remember

When I hear _____ I remember

When I see _____ I remember

When I touch _____ I remember

A Wave of Nostalgia

The smell that comes after a rain makes me think of

The taste of warm chocolate chip cookies makes
me think of

The sound of waves makes me think of

The sight of spring's first bird makes me think of

The feel of grass between my toes makes me think of

The smell of lilacs makes me think of

The taste of a roasted marshmallow makes me think of

The sound of an engine revving makes me think of

The sight of the color purple makes me think of

The feel of old wooden stairs beneath my feet makes
me think of

My earliest real-life crush

My earliest celebrity crush

My first kiss

My first bad kiss

A bad breakup

Near and Far

Write the years or decades of your life, evenly distributed, on the bottom of this graph. Plot the times when you felt closest to God and farthest from God.

Closeness to God

Years or Decades of Life

Near and Far

When I look at my life on the Near and Far graph,
I notice how

When I compare the Near and Far graph to the Ups and
Downs graph on page 52, I can draw these conclusions

The Soundtrack of My Life

Music is more than background noise. It's a universal language that is understood across time and culture. Cue up a song, and in an instant you can feel the urge to dance, cry, worship, or grab the karaoke mic. Your life has a soundtrack. Can you hear it?

If I could pick one song to sum up my life story, this is the one I'd pick

The Soundtrack of My Life

Your ability to answer this set of questions will depend on your generation. But if you're an old soul (or a young soul) you might have multiple, cross-generational answers. Let's give this a go.

The 8-track tape that ruled my world

The album that was scratched so badly it skipped

The cassette tape I played so much that it literally stopped working

The mix CD that moves me still

The Spotify playlist that is my go-to right now

The Soundtrack of My Life

A list of a few of my all-time favorite songs

The Soundtrack of My Life

A few of my favorite songs right now

In the Neighborhood

Recall a neighborhood/city/farm where you lived as a child. Draw everything you can remember about it. Don't forget your favorite climbing trees, streets, hiding places, hangouts, businesses, and the houses of your favorite (and least favorite) people.

I have laughed at these inappropriate times

I wish I could go back and change this

My past, summed up in three words

1. _____
2. _____
3. _____

The kindest, most loving thing I can do to make peace
with my past is

Me and My Right Now

So much of our lives is spent looking back at the *could-have-beens* and forward toward the *what-I-hope-will-be*. Yet, there is so much to see, experience, and learn right here and now.

It's a matter of being where your feet are. Here, there is no rehashing the past and no freaking out about the future. It's an invitation to be present with yourself and with God in this moment.

There are times to look back and remember. And there are times to plan for what is to come.

Today is simply a time to *be all here.*

If the little things in life are the most important things of all, these are the little things that matter most to me today

Here are things that I used to worry about that I don't anymore

Here are things that I didn't used to worry about that I do now

Here's what worries me today

My Heart of Thanks

Begin filling out the calendar on the next page at the start of a new month, keeping track of what you're grateful for every day, for a whole month.

CALENDAR

1	2	3	4	5
6	7	8	9	10
11	12	13	14	15
16	17	18	19	20
21	22	23	24	25
26	27	28	29	30
31	**notes:**			

Free Time

Divide the circle into a pie chart and add labels to show how you spend your free time. To get you started, consider time spent on cooking, hobbies, reading, shopping, exercising, socializing, napping, Netflix, social media, studying something that interests you, or anything else, other than required work. As you fill it out, think about whether you'd like to change anything about how you use free time.

These Are My Scars

Mark the body with your physical scars, and write down how you got them or what you feel when you see them.

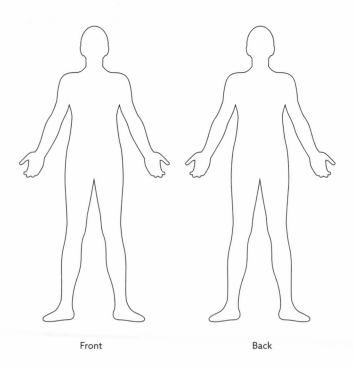

Front   Back

These Are My Scars

These are the scars I have that other people can't see, the ones from wounds on my heart and soul

Here are ways I know I'm healing, right now, from the wounds that caused these scars

Here are ways I know I still need to heal

Some ways I've grown lately

Some ways I've gotten worse

What I like about my body

What I like about my personality

What I like about my day-to-day

In the last week, this is when I experienced . . .

a moment of peace

a moment of disappointment

a moment of hopefulness

a moment of sorrow

a moment of silliness

a moment of confusion

a moment of surprise

a moment of regret

a moment of relief

Happiness Bingo

BINGO

Did something creative	Stepped outside	Ate healthy food	Sent a thoughtful text	Watched a sunset
Made a child laugh	Prayed for someone	Bought myself flowers	Drank more water	Took the scenic route
Forgave someone	Lit candles	FREE	Memorized a new Bible verse	Read a good book
Anonymously blessed someone	Ate dessert	Listened to music	Thanked someone	Washed the sheets
Celebrated a small win	Unplugged	Took a nap	Decluttered a closet	Watched a funny movie

Do the things that make you (and others) happy this month. Check off a square for each one accomplished.

These are the things I'm beginning to doubt

These are the things I'm beginning to believe

My life is valuable because

If I could ask God one question, this is what I'd ask

I'm going to do this spontaneous thing

Pray about Everything

"Don't worry about anything; instead, pray about everything. Tell God what you need, and thank him for all he has done" (Philippians 4:6 NLT).

Here is a running list of things I'm praying about right now (keep coming back to these pages and add more prayer requests as they come to mind)

This year I . . .

learned

loved

listened to

lamented

lifted up

laughed about

lacked

led

limited

looked at

left

longed for

lightened

lived like

If I knew I only had two weeks left to live

Here's a list of things I believe to be true about God

Here's a list of things I no longer believe to be true about God

Recharge

Here's when my body and soul are fully charged, at 100%

Here's when I need some recharging

Here's when I am completely on empty

Recharge

Here are some things I can do to stay charged

Here are some things that are sucking my battery life,
that I need to eliminate

My Faith Statement

If someone were to ask you what you believe, what would you want them to know? This is your chance to get it down on paper.

"And if someone asks about your hope as a believer, always be ready to explain it" (1 Peter 3:15 NLT).

A Pie Chart for My Feelings

Divide this pie chart into the appropriate sizes for your feelings during this season of your life, and insert the words that best represent what you've been feeling. A few emotions to get you thinking—happy, amused, sad, angry, disgusted, silly, lonely, hopeless, anxious, stressed, joyful, vengeful, delighted, astonished, afraid, bored.

A Pie Chart for My Interactions with God

Divide the following categories into a pie chart representing how you interact with God during a typical week. Use only the categories that apply.

Far from God   Delighting in God

Close to God   Talking to God

Ignoring God   Listening for God

Angry at God   Not thinking about God

This is what I've been daydreaming about lately

Me and My Places

Take a moment and think of all the places you've lived, visited, loved, and hated. Now we begin.

Of all the places in the world, this one most shaped
who I am right now

I never want to go here again

This is the place where I fell in love

I left a part of my heart here

Me and My Places

This is a place I visited that gave me a new perspective

I hope I can go here again one day

. . . and this is why

Me and My Places

A list of what I like about the place where I live now

A list of what I'd like to change about the place where I live now

Me and My Places

My Best Places

Best bookstore

Best park

Best local lunch joint

Best hiding spot

Best city

Best place for a one-day road trip

Best thinking spot

Best lake

Best place for a good bargain

Best coffee shop

Best place to pray

Best place for a picnic

Best hair salon

Best street

Best cemetery

Best place to escape

Best beach

Best place to get breakfast

Best neighborhood

Best place to fall in love

Me and My Places

Thin Places

Thin places are physical locations where the veil between heaven and earth seems very thin and porous. Here, you sense that you are in the middle of a sacred, transcendent place. You can breathe again. God is very near.

These are my thin places

Quick-Fire Favorites (and Least Favorites)

Favorite	Least Favorite
Cartoon character	
Store	
Season	
Coping mechanism	
Cereal	
Game	
Restaurant	
Song	
Villain	
Concert	
Prank	
Chore	
Ice cream flavor	
Distraction	

Quick-Fire Favorites
(and Least Favorites)

Favorite	Least Favorite
Way to cook an egg	
Holiday	
Candy	
Scent	
Gift to receive	
Schoolteacher	
Childhood picture book	
Commercial	
Bible verse	
Emoji	
Cure for the hiccups	
Sound	
Pair of shoes	
Question in this journal	

Seasons of My Life

Each season in the natural world serves its purpose.

Spring is a time of planting, a coming-alive season of hopefulness and beginnings.

Summer is a time of growth, when the warming world bursts forth in fruitfulness.

Fall is a time of harvest, when leaves fall and it's time to reap what has grown.

Winter is a time of rest, when the land goes quiet and the light of the sky dims.

This is the season that would best describe my life as it is right now (circle one):

Spring   Summer   Fall   Winter

Here's what I want to say to God about the season I'm in right now

Seasons of My Life

Here are times I've been in each of the four seasons . . .

My spring seasons

My summer seasons

My fall seasons

My winter seasons

What a privilege it is to be alive—here's how I want to make this day count

The kindest, most loving thing I can do for myself today is

Let Us Pray

Write down a prayer for right now

Me and My Weird Ways

People love to organize themselves into broad categories. Think the Enneagram, Myers-Briggs, Strengths-Finder, Buzzfeed quizzes, and many more. It feels good to learn a little more about yourself, and it brings comfort to know that you belong in a larger group of people with similar characteristics.

But as much as you want to fit in with a group, you also want to be unique. The great news is, you are.

Marvel at the fact that you are a one-of-a-kind, unrepeatable sequence of DNA. You were created as a Limited Edition, with your own personality traits, characteristics, preferences, habits, perspectives, and quirks.

Embrace your weird, wild, whimsical, well-made self. What makes you different is also what makes you wonderful.

The Venn Diagram of Weird, Wild, Whimsical, Well-Made Me

Let's celebrate that there is really only one you. Pick three hobbies, careers, interests, or facts about you that are uncommon to many people and place them on the diagram. Where the three converge, you'll find yourself—right in the middle of the Venn diagram. Odds are, that center spot is a spot that can only be filled by one person: you. The author of this journal will go first, so you get the idea.

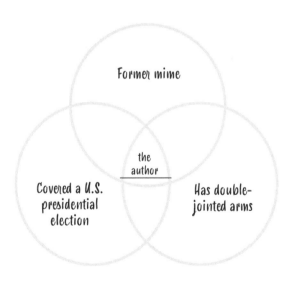

The Venn Diagram of Weird, Wild, Whimsical, Well-Made Me

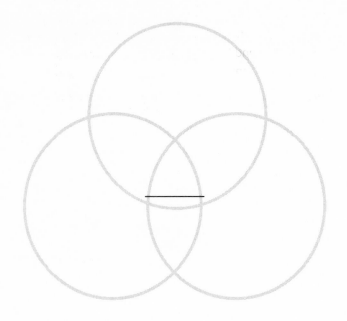

Unpopular Opinions

Unpopular opinions are ideas that contradict conventional points of view. Opinions like, "Living in the suburbs is better than living in the city." Or, "The TV show *Friends* is over-rated." Everybody's got unpopular opinions, but not everybody shares them because they don't want to face backlash from friends and family. Here's your chance to list yours, without judgment.

Here are my unpopular opinions about . . .

Food

TV

Unpopular Opinions

Movies

Relationships

Anything else

Three things I'm weirdly great at

1. ....
2. ....
3. _____

Three things I love that I'm embarrassed to share

1. _____
2. _____
3. ....

This is how I know that God has a sense of humor

Worst nightmare I've ever had

A dream from which I wish I hadn't woken up so early

A recurring dream I've had

My go-to "Two Truths and a Lie" statements

    Truth

    Truth

    Lie

If a toy manufacturer were to make an action figure of me, these are the three accessories it would come with

Stupid Human Tricks

For years, late-night TV host David Letterman used to bring regular people on the show to show off their "stupid human trick." They would get their fifteen seconds of fame by doing tricks like blowing up a balloon with their nose, Hula-Hooping while doing pull-ups, squirting milk out of their eye, juggling three apples and eating them at the same time, and so on. You get the point.

My stupid human trick

What are the five movies, five books, and five music albums you'd take if you were sent off to a desert island for a year? Write on the spines of the books, the records, and the film-reel tape.

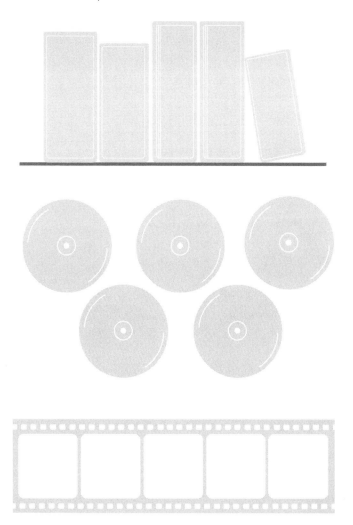

The weirdest thing I've ever eaten

The weirdest text I've ever gotten

The weirdest text I've ever sent

The weirdest job I've ever had

The weirdest person I've ever known

The weirdest place I've ever visited

If I had a superpower, it would be

If I could become invisible for a day, I would go

If I had the world's attention for an entire minute, this is what I'd say

The word I always misspell (*or is it mispell?*)

The most useless skill I possess

The most useful skill I possess

This part of my fourteen-year-old self is the part that embarrasses me most

The best gift I've ever given somebody was

The best gift I've ever received was

The worst gift I've ever received was

Yes or No

Y or N   I would survive a zombie apocalypse

Y or N   I consider myself funny

Y or N   I like myself

Y or N   I fear intimacy

Y or N   I'm too liberal for most people

Y or N   I'm too conservative for most people

Y or N   I'm too liberal for some people and too conservative for some people

Y or N   Public speaking scares me

Y or N   I've peed in the woods

Y or N   I've shoplifted

Y or N   I still sleep with a stuffed toy or childhood blanket

Y or N   I am afraid of dreaming

Y or N   I have prank-called someone

Y or N   I have gone skinny-dipping

Y or N   Dying scares me

Y or N   I can change the oil in my car

Y or N   I believe other beings exist elsewhere in the universe

Y or N   I often feel misunderstood

My Leitmotif

A leitmotif is a short musical phrase that accompanies the appearance of a figure or person in entertainment, like operas and movies. For instance, the shark in *Jaws* has his own shark music to signal his appearance. Let's say that from now until the day you die, the same song came on every time you walked into a room. What song would you want it to be?

My leitmotif is

This is my full name

And this is what I think of it

As far as I know, this is why I have that name

If I could have any other name in the world, this is the
one I'd pick

If I were a spy, my code name would be

Weirdest thing in my purse or wallet

A word in my native language that always makes
me chuckle

A word in my native language that always makes
me cringe

My dream last meal is

This or That

sweet OR savory

early riser OR night owl

spring OR autumn

coffee OR tea

Mac OR PC

mystery OR romance

texting OR phone call

mountain OR beach

sunrise OR sunset

Whole Foods OR Trader Joe's

music OR silence

plans OR spontaneity

dinner with friends OR night alone

how I think OR how I feel

change-loving OR change-averse

cook a meal OR order carryout

Twizzlers OR Red Vines

If I got a tattoo, this is what it would look like

These are three songs that, when I hear them, get stuck in my head all day long

1. ....

2. ....

3. ....

(Oh, sorry about that)

The seven most beautiful things I've ever seen are

1. _____
2. _____
3. _____
4. _____
5. _____
6. _____
7. _____

I can't believe God let me witness this

If I could start a secret society, I'd call it this

The last thing I did for fun was this

What Do You See in Me?

Cut these pages out and give them to someone you love. Ask them to answer these questions about you and then give it back.

What I see in _____ (insert name here)

Describe their best quality

Describe their perfect day

What Do You See in Me?

What are they most proud of?

Where would we go on a vacation together?

Something weird about this person that I hope
never changes

What Do You See in Me?

What this person is most afraid of

Something I want this person to know when they are having a hard day

This is what our relationship means to me

What Do You See in Me?

Here is something that surprised me about this person, as we got to know each other more

This is my favorite memory of us together

When can we hang out again?

Here I will draw something that makes me happy

Here I will draw something I miss

The worst date I've ever been on

The best date I've ever been on

The date that sounds 110 percent perfect

If my house were burning down, this is what I'd grab before I left

This is what the world would be like if it were populated by clones of me

The most interesting thing I've learned this week

The best purchase I've ever made

The worst purchase I've ever made

LOST IN TRANSLATION, PART II

(Find other "Lost in Translation" sections on pages 24–29 and pages 178–180.)

Bilita Mpash, Bantu

Bilita Mpash is the opposite of a nightmare. It's more than just a good dream. It's a legendary one, the kind you'd want to have over and over again.

Here's my most excellent *bilita mpash*

Shemomedjamo, Georgian

You know that feeling you get when you are eating something really delicious, and you are so full, but you keep eating anyway? That's *shemomedjamo*.

This was a moment of *shemomedjamo* for me, and I'm not sorry about it

LOST IN TRANSLATION

> ### *Waldeinsamkeit*, German
> *Waldeinsamkeit* is translated loosely as solitude in the woods.
> It's a word that describes that peaceful, calm, sublime feeling
> of solitude you get when you are present amidst the trees.
> You might have felt a form of it any time you experienced a
> connection with nature.

This is a time when I experienced *waldeinsamkeit*

> ### *Commuovere*, Italian
> *Commuovere* is the way you are deeply touched and moved
> to tears, often by a heartwarming, beautiful story.

Here's a story that evokes *commuovere* in me

Hygge, Danish

Hygge is that cozy, comfortable feeling you get in a warm, inviting atmosphere, especially enjoying good things with good people. Cozying up around a fire in the winter is _hygge_. The soft glow of candlelight at the dinner table is _hygge_.

This is a sketch of a time when I felt the coziness of _hygge_

As Honest As I've Ever Been

You've spent some valuable time exploring the fun, playful, wild, and wonderful ways God made you. That's the magic of taking time to record all that comes to mind when you think about "Me and My Weird Ways."

And now, you've turned the page to find yourself here. You'll notice a shift in tone here, where we begin the hard work of deep introspection. This is the section where the rubber meets the road.

This is the section you might never want to share with anyone.

But don't run from these pages. These are the ones of beautifully ruthless self-discovery.

Push yourself. Dig deep. Take off every disguise. Let yourself explore what you've never been brave enough to explore before.

Yes, this takes work.

But it may be the most important work you'll do.

It's where you get as honest as you've ever been.

Sometimes I don't want to get out of bed because

I've been most angry at these three times in my life

Here are my honest feelings about God letting bad things happen in the world

This is the struggle that most shaped who I am today

Addictions

Addiction comes in many forms. Some addictions are obvious—when they come in a bottle or a needle or on a casino gaming floor. Others are more easily hidden but cause harm in other ways: shopping, approval, exercise, food, productivity, career advancement.

This is something I'm addicted to

This is something I'm afraid I'll become addicted to

Addictions

This is a prayer I can pray to ask God to get me free (and keep me free) from addiction

This is an action I can take today to put distance between me and my addiction

When I am feeling especially sad, these are ten healthy things I do (or can do) to regain a bit of joy

1. _____

   _____

2. _____

   _____

3. _____

   _____

4. _____

   _____

5. _____

   _____

6. _____

   _____

7. _____

   _____

8. _____

   _____

9. _____

   _____

10. _____

    _____

Life is a combination of unwanted delays, hoped-for things that never come to pass, and, happily, some serendipitous moments that unfold right on time. If an airport flight status monitor were tracking your life, it would be a combination of all three of those things: delays, cancellations, and on-time arrivals.

The airport flight monitor status of my life

DEPARTURES	STATUS	ARRIVALS	STATUS
	Delayed		Delayed
	Canceled		Canceled
	On Time		On Time
	Delayed		Delayed
	Canceled		Canceled
	On Time		On Time
	Delayed		Delayed
	Canceled		Canceled
	On Time		On Time
	Delayed		Delayed
	Canceled		Canceled
	On Time		On Time

For the Hard Days

This is what I'd want myself to know on a hard day. I will brain dump it here (my future self will thank me).

For the Hard Days

On a hard day, this is how I know God loves me

On a hard day, I need to remember that these people care about me

On a hard day, I need God to comfort me by

On a hard day, these are the truths I need to be reminded of

Come back to these pages on a hard day.

These Bible verses scare me

These Bible promises blow my mind

These Bible verses have saved me

Facing Your Fears

Fear is one of the most powerful, complex emotions of the lived human experience. Today's as good a day as any to face what scares you the most—and to take a few steps toward finding the things that are stronger than your fears.

A fear I have that others find irrational

This is a way that fear was helpful and kept me safe

A time that fear held me back

A fear I have about the future

Facing Your Fears

A fear that I later discovered was unfounded

This is a fear I have today, and this is the worst possible scenario

. . . and this is the best possible scenario

. . . and this is the most likely scenario

A fear I faced with great courage

Facing Your Fears

A fear I'd like to overcome, and this is how my life might be different if I could

These are the words I would say to someone else with that same fear

This is one step I can take to begin to tackle this fear

Here's how I need God to help me with my fear

If I were God I would

The thing that surprises me most about God is

If I had veto power when God created the world I would

I was most mad at God when

These are things I need to let go of

These are things I need to hold on to

Here are the most hurtful words someone has said to me

Here are some affirmations or truths I can speak to heal
the wounds caused by those hurtful words

These are the things that confuse me about . . .

my parents

my personality

my community

my past

These are the things that confuse me about . . .

my behaviors

my circumstances

my future

God

I know I'm supposed to believe _____
_____,
but I'm not sure I do

This is the thing that makes me most likely to not
believe in God

This is the thing that always reassures me that God is
absolutely real

This is the thing that often keeps me from sharing
my faith

A list of ways that I hold back in my life

1. _____

_____

_____

2. _____

_____

_____

3. _____

_____

_____

4. _____

_____

_____

5. _____

_____

_____

The Worst Day of My Life

The Best Day of My Life

Conversations with Jesus

Jesus was an asker of provocative questions. Throughout the gospels, he asked direct questions of people he encountered. If he were in the room with you today and asked you some of his questions, how would you answer them?

"Do you understand what I have done for you?" (John 13:12)

My answer

"Why are you troubled, and why do doubts rise in your minds?" (Luke 24:38)

My answer

"Do you want to get well?" (John 5:6)

My answer

Conversations with Jesus

"What do you want me to do for you?" (Luke 18:41)

My answer

"Why did you doubt?" (Matthew 14:31)

My answer

"You do not want to leave too, do you?" (John 6:67)

My answer

Conversations with Jesus

"When the Son of Man comes, will he find faith on the earth?"
(Luke 18:8)

My answer

"Why are you so afraid?" (Matthew 8:26)

My answer

"Do you still not see or understand?" (Mark 8:17)

My answer

"Do you love me?" (John 21:17)

My answer

If I Were a Psalmist

Flip through the Psalms. They are filled with celebration, feasting, and unbridled shouts of joy. They are also the uncensored, unfiltered cries of people with broken hearts. Imagine the anguish as they asked questions like

How long, O Lord?

Where are you?

Why have you forsaken me?

These questions are not polite. They are raw and gritty. If you were a psalmist, in a moment of lament, what would you cry out to God? If you were a psalmist, in a moment of praise, what would you want the world to know?

Now, it's your turn to find out.

If I Were a Psalmist

Here Is My Psalm of Lament

How long, O Lord? Why do you hide yourself from me in this time of

How long must I

How long until you

I cry out to you, O God. Give ear to my prayer. (Here, tell God how difficult things are right now. Be as specific as you can be about the circumstances that trouble you.)

My longings are before you, Lord. Hear my cry.

If I Were a Psalmist

Here Is My Psalm of Praise

Come, let us sing to the Lord!

Let us shout joyfully to the Lord, for he is _____ and
_____ (adjectives that describe God's character)

The Lord is a great God, for he has given us

I see God's goodness in

My spirit yearns to praise the Lord, our God. I give joyous
thanks for

LOST IN TRANSLATION, PART III

(Find other "Lost in Translation" sections on pages 24–29 and pages 143–145.)

Kummerspeck, German

Literally, *kummerspeck* translates to "grief bacon." It's a term to describe weight gained due to emotional overeating.

I suffered from *kummerspeck* when

Schadenfreude, German

Schadenfreude is a combination of two words. *Schaden* means damage; *freude* means joy. So *schadenfreude* is the joy you feel at another person's pain, like the way you might feel when someone who passed you on the road, then cut in front of you, gets pulled over by the police a mile later. Or when someone accused of a violent crime is hauled off to jail. Or maybe something a little closer to home, if you're willing to admit it.

I felt a sense of *schadenfreude* in my gut when this happened

LOST IN TRANSLATION

Saudade, Portuguese

Saudade is a longing or nostalgia for someone who is absent, something you may never have experienced—or may never experience again.

I have been in a state of *saudade* when

Wabi-sabi, Japanese

Wabi-sabi is the concept of finding and appreciating beauty in imperfection.

Perfection is overrated. I'm finding *wabi-sabi* right here

. . . and right here

. . . and right here

LOST IN TRANSLATION

Now, it's your turn. Think of an emotion you've felt or a reaction you've had, for which there is no good English word, and then make up your own name and definition for it.

Name

Definition

How I Feel

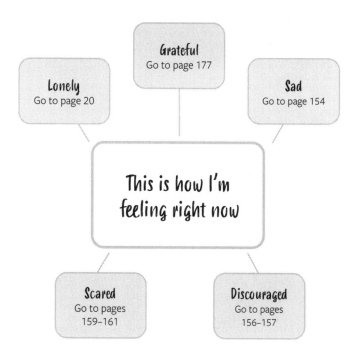

Grateful
Go to page 177

Lonely
Go to page 20

Sad
Go to page 154

This is how I'm
feeling right now

Scared
Go to pages
159–161

Discouraged
Go to pages
156–157

Me and My Future

You can't go back and change what already happened, but you can begin again as you move toward life's ending. You can make a change. You can start doing what matters and stop doing what you hate. You can end a bad habit and pick up a good one.

You can dream. You can wonder. You can tell God what scares you about your future, and you can ask for him to lead you in paths he wants you to go.

The future is here. What are you waiting for?

I vow to do this

Tomorrow

Next week

Next month

My Bucket List

These are the things I want to do before I die, before I "kick the bucket"

My Anti-Bucket List

These are the things I'd never try, or that I've done before but will never do again (examples: tile a floor, eat pickled herring, stay in a toxic relationship, tattoo your lover's name on your arm)

I never want to see

This is the part of me I'm afraid will never change

Something I want to happen, but I'm afraid it won't

I would be happier if

If I could time travel, forward or backward, this is where I'd go

My Dream Vacation

If money and time were no object, I'd love to vacation here

I would go with

The view would include

This would be on the menu

My Dream Vacation

In the mornings, I would

In the afternoons, I would

In the evenings, I would

My mind would be focused on

I would be most captivated by

My Dream House

Draw what it looks like and describe it in as much detail as you like

I Want to See the World—Or Maybe I Don't

Color green the places you want to see.
Color blue the places you have been.
Color red the places you never want to go.

What does your world map tell you about yourself?

Procrastination Station

It's time for a brain dump. Here's a place to think through a few things you've been putting off—the big and little things. Things like asking for a raise, making that recipe you've had saved for three years on Pinterest, booking the vacation you've been meaning to book, confronting the friend you've needed to confront, painting the room you've wanted to paint, making the confession you need to make.

Brain dump it here

Here's why I've been putting these things off

Now go back and circle at least one that you'll act on within the next seven days.

My Habits

There are two kinds of habits—the bad habits that hold us back and the good habits that move us forward. Today's as good a day as any to make a change that will move you in the direction you want to go.

Pick your journey.

This is a habit I want to end
OR
This is a habit I want to begin

This is why this change is important to me

My Habits

Here is something I can do today to make that change

Here is an accountability person I trust to keep me moving forward

Here's a list of the possible people or circumstances that threaten my forward growth

My Habits

This is where I feel especially weak and need God's help

I would like to reach this goal in thirty days

This is how I will celebrate on day thirty-one

Progress Chart

I will chart my first thirty days of progress on the next page. In charting my progress, I pledge to celebrate the big and small victories that will happen, give myself grace if it didn't work out as I hoped, and vow to start again because this is important to me.

Sign your name here to accept this pledge and vow

_____

My Habits

In each box, make a small note of victories, grace needed, and strength required to begin again. You got this.

CALENDAR				
1	2	3	4	5
6	7	8	9	10
11	12	13	14	15
16	17	18	19	20
21	22	23	24	25
26	27	28	29	30
notes:				

If I could bring a person who has died back into my life, this is who it would be

. . . and this is why

If I could bring a person who is still living back into my life, this is who it would be

. . . and this is why

When I am old, I'm afraid I'll forget

When I am old, these are the stories that children will ask me about

Adult MASH

MASH is the classic kids' game where you predict your future—who you'll marry, (this can be anyone—a celebrity, someone who's dead or alive, someone you know, or a perfect stranger) where you'll live, and so on. Don't take this too seriously. It's just a game, after all. Let's play.

Step 1:

MASH

List four possible life partners

List four cities or places to live

List four types of vehicles

List four possible jobs

Adult MASH

Step 2: Close your eyes and draw a spiral for eight seconds. Count from the outside the number of lines you drew, like this.

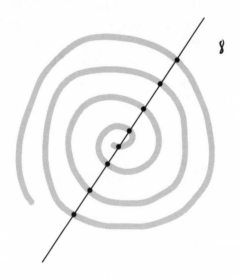

Here's my number:

Step 3: Starting with the letters M, A, S, and H near the top of the previous page, begin counting and go, in order, through each of the options until you hit the magic number. Cross off the option on the previous page that matches the magic number.

Step 4: Start counting at the next option, and keep going until you hit the magic number again. Cross that option off. Repeat until you have only one option in each category.

Adult MASH

Step 5: Circle the one remaining option in each category (the example here shows additional categories you could try if you play again).

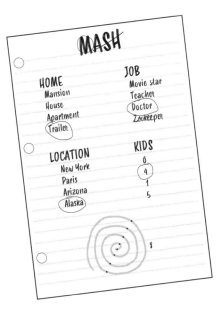

Here's my MASH story

I'm going to spend the rest of my life with

We will drive a

. . . and live in

My job will be

Money Matters

This is what I would buy if money were no object

This is what I would buy with my last ten dollars

Money Matters

Growing up, this is how I learned to see money (check all that apply):

- ☐ There's never enough
- ☐ The love of money is the root of all evil
- ☐ Money is a tool that will get you what you want
- ☐ Time is more valuable than money
- ☐ Money can buy you happiness
- ☐ Money can't buy you happiness
- ☐ Money = Freedom
- ☐ Money = Enslavement
- ☐ It takes money to make money
- ☐ Money is a blessing
- ☐ No one has ever become poor by giving money to someone who needs it
- ☐ Money can't buy you love
- ☐ Never spend money you don't have
- ☐ Save, save, save
- ☐ *Add yours below*

Money Matters

This is my philosophy on money today

I wish I could afford to hire someone to do this

This is what I hope my financial future looks like

A list of books I want to read (write on the book spines)

I dream of learning how to

I dream of getting to know

I dream of being able to afford

I dream of reuniting with

I dream of getting over

I dream of meeting this famous person

I dream of gaining the courage to

I dream of making amends with

I dream of a world where

I dream of becoming better at

I dream of giving myself grace for

I dream of helping

I dream of changing

I dream of fixing

I dream of understanding

I dream of visiting

This is what I want a day in my life to look like a year from today

The End of Here

"LORD, remind me how brief my time on earth will be. Remind me that my days are numbered—how fleeting my life is" (Psalm 39:4 NLT).

This is what goes through my mind when I think about dying

This would be the worst way to die

This is the way I prefer to die

If I am buried, I want to be buried with

If I am cremated, I want my ashes to be spread here

The End of Here

If I could have any songs played at my funeral, and no one had veto power, these are the ones I'd pick

These are the things I hope get talked about at my funeral

This is what I want my tombstone to look like

A New Beginning

"In My Father's house are many mansions; if it were not so, I would have told you. I go to prepare a place for you" (John 14:2 NKJV).

This is what goes through my mind when I think about heaven

This is who I hope will meet me when I first get there

This is what I hope God says to me

This person/group of people might be surprised I'm there

A New Beginning

I hope that heaven includes:

fields overflowing with

conversations centering around

choirs singing about

days filled with

houses furnished with

rivers flowing with

a twenty-four-hour buffet with the following food

daily chats with people from the Bible, especially

a matinee that features the best moments of my life,
such as

A New Beginning

When I imagine myself in heaven, I see myself as
(think of your personality, appearance, age, etc.)

This is what I think I'll do the moment I see Jesus
face-to-face

Finally

Congratulations. You have filled more than two hundred pages with the stuff you'd only tell God.

Honestly? Some of your truths were easy to tell, the kind of stuff you'd disclose to a friend, or even a stranger.

But much of what you wrote took great courage.

You know yourself a little better than you did before, and that's no small thing.

And here's something that may come as a surprise. The stuff you'd only tell God—is the stuff he already knew. He even knows the parts you didn't write down. *Yet.*

There's a chance to tell more, you know.

You can do this all over again, and when you do, you will excavate even deeper than before. You will uncover answers you didn't find the first time because

- you and your people keep changing
- you and your relationship with your past keep changing
- your weird ways are always changing
- how honest you'll get will continue changing
- your "right now" is always, always changing
- how you feel about your future will change, too.

Before you go, it's time to make some vows. This is an opportunity to take decisive action on what you've learned about yourself on these pages. Let's go.

My Vows

Three things I'm going to do to:

Improve my mind

Be better in relationships

Draw closer to God

Live healthier

Accept myself

Offer grace

My Vows

I'll forgive myself for

I'll forgive _____ for

I'll take time to

I'll remember that

I'll finish

If, when I'm gone, someone finds this journal tucked away in its hiding place, this is what I want them to know most of all

A Final Challenge

Do you know what's braver than telling your secrets to God? Sharing your secrets with someone who doesn't already know them. The next step is to tell your stuff to your people. Go through *Stuff I'd Only Tell God* again, this time with a friend, sibling, or significant other.

You're just getting started.

Write down the name of one person you might be brave enough to tell

A Parting Blessing

"The Lord bless you and keep you; the Lord make His face shine upon you, and be gracious to you; the Lord lift up His countenance upon you, and give you peace."

Numbers 6:24–26 NKJV

Jennifer Dukes Lee is a fan of queso, bright lipstick, and singing too loudly to songs with great harmony. A former news reporter nicknamed "Scoop Dukes," she loves asking tough questions. Her friends say they are scared to sit alone in a room with her because they end up telling her things they never intended to say. She is both proud of this fact and also a little annoyed by her persistent nosiness. She lives on a fifth-generation family farm in Iowa, where she and her husband have made a life of growing crops, pigs, two beautiful humans, and an enduring faith that makes room for questions.

Follow Jennifer on social media @jenniferdukeslee. She dares you to share your journal pages on Instagram and TikTok. Use the hashtag #StuffIdOnlyTellGod.